Slow Surrender

Lindsay Reid

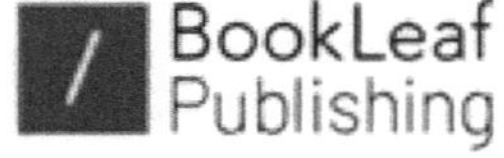

Slow Surrender © 2022 Lindsay Reid

All rights reserved.

No part of this publication may be reproduced, stored in a retrieval system, or transmitted, in any form or by any means, electronic, mechanical, photocopying, recording or otherwise, without the prior written permission of the presenters.

Lindsay Reid asserts the moral right to be identified as author of this work.

Presentation by *BookLeaf Publishing*

Web: www.bookleafpub.com

E-mail: info@bookleafpub.com

ISBN: 9789357210928

First edition 2022

PREFACE

I have not found these last few years easy; a pandemic bringing isolation due to immunosuppression, several hospitalisations, a loss of mobility, and a great deal of pain.

These poems have been my way of trying to trust God, even when it feels like my life is falling apart. I am convinced that He is faithful and I believe that He has been teaching me in the difficulties - even though at the time, the suffering sometimes feels pointless.

As I learn to rely on Him more and more each day, knowing that on my own I can't go on, I see the many blessings He has given me, particularly in the people he has placed in my life.

I hope that these poems comfort you, perhaps reflecting some of your own cries of 'Why?' to God. I pray that God would be glorified in my writing and may He strengthen and encourage you as you read.

Slow Surrender

My loss hurts me less than my thwarted will.
The weakness of my body is easier to accept
In abstract terms – when it prevents me
From doing as I please, I burn with anger.

What does it mean? Lord, why should I
Be trusted to die in this way? How can I bear it?
Not my will, but yours. Yet how is this
Your will? You place in my heart a passion

And then thwart it, time and again. It makes
No sense. Maybe there are grander purposes
But stuck on earth in this failing body
I cannot see them.

Why no grand steps of faith for me?
Only a slow surrender to pain, only a child
Crying for a parent to help because she
Doesn't understand, she can't do this alone.

It is not 'only' a slow surrender. Perhaps
The surrender is all – to fall
Into the Father's arms, to find my purpose
In Him. To trust that He knows best.

What can be borne

And some Psalms
end in the darkness.
Well, one Psalm.
One in one hundred and fifty.
Do you think that means
one in one hundred and fifty
Christians' stories
end in the dark?

I know some do.
And all we learn
is that this is
a broken world
and we are
a fallen people.
Some songs end in
A minor key.

Some stories fail
to end in triumph.
And yet love remains -
Forgiveness too.
I love you. Forgive me.
I am loved and forgiven
and still I cannot
bear to live.

Psalm 118:17

3

I will not die but
live and proclaim what my God
has done in my life.

Gentle

How do the gentle
survive in this world?
Buffeted by cruelty
harsh words and
indifference.

I am baffled as I see
their kindness
and more, their
vulnerability,
for to be gentle

is to be open
to the world,
to be willing to
receive its bruises,
to accept them

without fighting
back, without
retaliating. And yet
the gentle can be
so fierce –

They stay with those
in pain. They care.
They do not let go.
They do not leave.
They love.

And I realised
at long last
that gentleness
is really strength
held back.

Daily Exercise

Each morning I give
you to God. Each evening I
try to take you back.

Undying

7

Bereaved. Bereft.
We're left to mourn
For these our children
Lost, unborn,
Stillborn, like buds
On roses never
To open or
To flower, ever.

But oh, the thorns —
The thorns that cling
To eyes, to heart,
To everything —
Please save us, Lord.
We cannot bear
The thorns that pierce
And stab and tear.

Please gather us
That some day, we
Will meet those lost
To us and see

How all the sorrow
Comes untrue
The unborn child
Is born anew

And every heart
Is healed and whole
And there is light
In every soul
And there is hope
In every eye,
For here His children
Cannot die.

Hard Birth

It was a long, hard birth -
ten years or more.

You felt the pain
of confusion and heartache,
struggling to make sense of it all.

And all of us around you
crying 'Why? Why?'
when you did not recognize us,
your mind shattered beyond repair.

It was a long, hard birth.

That struggle to leave
one world
to enter the next.

You gained a glimpse of the hell
you would escape.

It was a long, hard birth.
We watched you go.
It tore our hearts in two

and yet we know that now
you're home at last,
pain long forgotten,

whole and happy,
you're singing holy praises
to the Lord who saved your soul.

It was a long, hard birth,
but a birth worth waiting for.

Good Friday

And as you hung
From those crossed beams

Splitting history in two
With each blood-flecked breath

The stars splintered
And the stones wept aloud.

In Paradise

He is my Lord and He is hanging
on the cross once again
as He does every Good Friday.
I see Him. His back flayed to ribbons.
The nails. The thorns.

'Father, forgive them
for they know not
what they do.'

He is forgiving them again
as He always does in this
timeless, cosmic drama
played out against a backdrop
of ordinary people.

'This day you
will be with me
in paradise.'

He tenderly tells the thief
hanging beside Him –
and then He looks out
over the broken world,
offers us the same.

Call of the Stars

Can you hear the starlight? From a million
miles away
It sings across the universe and causes men
to pray.
When you hear the music, you will never be
the same -
You cannot help but follow when a star calls
out your name.

If you hear the starlight, you will end up set
apart,
Knowing something great and terrible has
happened to your heart,
A wounding or igniting - both alike will
touch your soul -
You'll be broken into pieces, and the pain
will make you whole.

Day Seven

He was not surprised
when the virus took hold.
Of course, we were.
We hadn't expected this –
hadn't expected disaster
to come on us suddenly.

He was not surprised
and he looked down with
tears in his eyes,
longing to gather us
as a hen gathers her chicks
under her wing.

He looked down on us in love
(watching our panicked scurries -
ants whose anthill is destroyed)
and he knew our fragile form
He knew we were dust
He knew the heart of man
and he was not surprised.

He was not surprised
because the world is groaning -
pandemics happen

heartaches happen
and he catches our tears
in a bottle.

He was not surprised
at our weakness,
at our frailty,
He knew it because
He has been among us
been one of us.

And now, as our world
hurtles towards crisis point
and we are locked down
in our own homes (the lucky ones)
and as we cry out to Him to save us
He was not surprised
and He will.

Afterwards

Washed up on the shore of my life
After battling an ocean of pain,
Everything looks like before
But it isn't the same.

Now that the sea has receded
I finally stand on dry land
Alone and shivering, I whisper
'This was not what I planned'.

But then I see on the horizon
The sun sets in glory and flame
My body is fragile and broken
But still, I am bearing His name

And He will return for his loved ones
I will not be left here alone
The dawn will sweep down like a chariot
And one day He'll carry me home.

Refining

It occurs to me
That I have become
Too good at suffering.

In every circumstance
My first impulse
Is to endure.

But what if I am just
Playing into old patterns,
Making it easy

To believe myself
A victim in this – that
I have no agency?

Ah, but how to change?
How to believe
That sometimes

These hardships thrown
At us by life are
The very things

That shape us
And turn us into
Something beautiful?

Burning

My lungs are red roses
I choke out petals

My heart is a butterfly
Fluttering dully

My gut is a snake
It writhes and bites

My mind is an ocean
Endlessly tossing

But my soul is a star
Burning bright.

Holy

In maze-like days my thoughts lie drowned
Pitch-dark, unfathomable and bleak,
Unkind, unseen, they seep to dreams
And whisper in each word I speak -

I am terrible, horrible, heart-deep ugly,
Selfish, uncaring, disgusting, cruel,
I could gouge my eyes out for what they've seen,
And scrape out my heart with a sharpened tool.

I could tear my flesh and burn my bones,
And crumple and twist and melt my mind,
And still the horrors that haunt my nights
Would remain in my splinters, left behind.

There is just one hope: the white-blinding pure
Cleansing of Jesus, for He alone
Can soothe my soul, piece me back together,
A heart of flesh, not a heart of stone.

He whispers His everlasting love,
And sends me friends who murmur to me
Truths that He gave them – they take my hand
And tell me who they can really see.

They let me know I am not alone –
That now I am holy. You never know.
Perhaps one day I will believe them.
One day. Perhaps. Pray it will be so.

Therefore we do not lose heart

Though outwardly
we are wasting away
yet inwardly
we are being renewed
day by day

For our light and
momentary troubles
are achieving for us
an eternal glory
that far outweighs them all

So we fix our eyes
not on what is seen
but on what is unseen
since what is seen is temporary
but what is unseen is eternal.

Invisible

21

I look into the invisible and see
beyond our gritty dull reality
green hope dances -
Child, the unseen grows in you:

Love rooted in your heart -
a thorn shaped seed
stretching out tendrils
through your grimy life

shaping and transforming
with agonising slowness
readying you for a land beyond
all you can see and know.

I will see

I cannot write to you, Lord,
as I used to write.
Things have become
more complicated

and I'm not just talking
about the pain.
I feel lost.
I feel like a little child.

Maybe that shows
I am growing up.
No more trite answers
or easy explanations.

My dreams have not
come true. My pain is
unrelenting. Suffering
is all around me.

Yet I have hope
when I think of this:
I will see your goodness
in the land of the living.

The worship of cats

My cats are teaching me
to worship You
as I observe them
going about
their daily lives.

When they lie in the sun
turning their bellies to the sky
stretching luxuriously
they are delighting
in your good gifts.

When they direct me
with plaintive meows
to their food bowl
they trust that what they need
will be provided.

When they play
with a ball or a leaf
or a cardboard box
they are not afraid
for the future.

When they sleep
in my lap, they purr,
letting me know
how thoroughly
satisfied they are.

They are fully present
and utterly themselves.
They live contentedly
knowing instinctively
they are loved.

Blessed

Of all people,
I have been most blessed.

Do not be sad.

I have seen such sights.
I have swum in blue, blue waters
in caves in Greece.
I have swum among coral reefs in India,
I have swum out to a great, hulking
iron wreck and climbed up it and
leapt off into the water.
I have skinny dipped in warm seas
beneath the stars,
I have braved English beaches
pebbly and cold, or sandy and
colder still –
lakes in Germany, rivers in Poland
I have been most blessed.

I have climbed such heights.
Hiking up the mountain in India
after sleeping around a fire,
the majestic heights of the Alps –
the Schilthorn and
Trummelbach falls,
the Pyrenees at sunset,
skiing down a mountainside,

hiking up mountains in Wales, in Spain,
travelling through mountains in Canada – Banff,
travelling on the train in Canada –
I have never known such luxury;
travelling on the train in India, with
the bare bunks and the bars at the windows
and the piping hot chai in the mornings,

I hold all these places in my heart:
The canals of Venice,
the silver stone and blue sea of St. Andrews,
the highlands of Scotland,
the hills of Shropshire where little
Ashtree Cottage nestled,
the storms over the vineyards
in the South of France,
the Yorkshire moors where the
Brontes wandered,
the ever-changing Solent,
the red and green hills of Ooty
where I left a piece of my heart,
the green and gold of dear Durham
that place of safety and freedom and hope –
and now this northern city, this
Newcastle of the bridges and the river and
the mouth of the Tyne and
the kindness I have found here,

I hold this beauty in my heart and
it is the best of me,
I have wandered some small part of
the world and all this was leading me home –
to a place far more beautiful, more alive, more free.

Do not be sad.

If the pilgrim reaches her
destination and the long journey is
over, it is only that there are new
lands to discover, greater joys to
experience, greater beauty ahead.

I glimpse the great beyond in the
beauty here and my heart cries out
for the eternal glory, endless beauty
ahead. I am not afraid. I know who
travels with me, who is before me
and behind me and waiting to
welcome me home.

Unheroic

As a lover of stories
I wanted my life to be heroic
Adventuring on the high seas
Fighting dragons
Rescuing those in distress

My story would have been
An epic - enchantments
Wizards, witches, faeries,
Beasts and monsters -
The whole shebang

And then I discover
My story is very different
To what I imagined.
It is quiet, unadventurous,
I stay at home a lot -

I'm not even sure that I am
The hero. I seem to be
The one in distress,
Relying on others
To rescue me.

It's a blow. We're told
We can forge our own paths
Write our own stories
But then the unexpected
Tornado swirls in.

Lately I have been
Wondering if this is really
My story at all. Maybe
I am a very minor character
In an epic story

A tale told since before
The dawn of time which
Will not be complete until
The earth is folded up
And put aside

And if that is the case
If my battles are unheroic
And behind the scenes
If my life can be summed up
In a few lines

Does that mean it is not
Meaningful? That my life is
Unimportant? All I know
Is that if I am in the story
Part of a masterpiece

Constructed by a genius
Beyond the boundaries of
What I can understand -
(Although I can see that
It is very beautiful

Despite the awful bits) -
All I need to do is
Faithfully play my part
Knowing that all things
Will come right in the end.

www.ingramcontent.com/pod-product-compliance
Lightning Source LLC
LaVergne TN
LVHW021333200726
843509LV00014B/2515